NATIONAL GEOGRAPHIC
Reach
for Reading
COMMON CORE PROGRAM

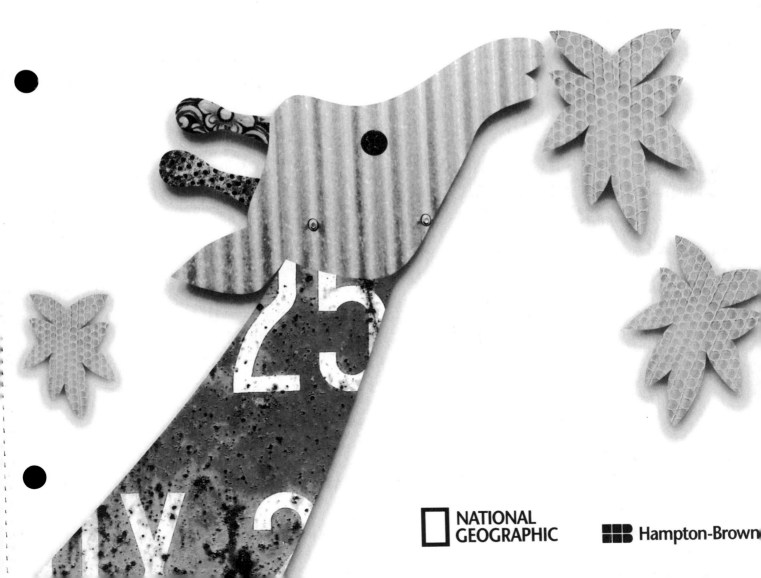

NATIONAL
GEOGRAPHIC

Hampton-Brown

Acknowledgments
Grateful acknowledgment is given to the authors, artists, photographers, museums, publishers, and agents for permission to reprint copyrighted material. Every effort has been made to secure the appropriate permission. If any omissions have been made or if corrections are required, please contact the Publisher.

Cover Design and Art Direction: Visual Asylum

Cover Illustration: Joel Sotelo

Illustration Credits: All PM illustrations by National Geographic Learning.

Visit National Geographic Learning online at www.NGSP.com

Visit our corporate website at www.cengage.com

Printed in the USA.

Printer: RR Donnelley, Harrisonburg, VA

ISBN: 978-11338-99594

12 13 14 15 16 17 18 19 20 21

10 9 8 7 6 5 4 3 2 1

Contents

Unit 1: My Family

Unit 2: Shoot for the Sun

Unit 3: To Your Front Door

Unit 4: Growing and Changing

Phonics

Letter and Sound Mm

Write the missing letter. Color each item named in the sentence.

1. m op	**2.** an	**3.** ask
4. ouse	**5.** ilk	**6.** itt
7. oon	**8.** at	**9.** ap

Read It Together   Find the man and the mat.

PM1.1

Unit 1 | My Family

Phonics

Letter and Sound Ss

Ss

Write the missing letter. Color each item named in the sentence.

1. soap	**2.** __ilk	**3.** __un
4. __ink	**5.** __eed	**6.** __ock
7. __eal	**8.** __ix	**9.** __even

Read It Together   Find the sun and the six.

Phonics

Letter and Sound Hh

Write the missing letter. Color each item named in the sentence.

1. h at	**2.** ook	**3.** un
4. ask	**5.** an	**6.** ose
7. and	**8.** ouse	**9.** orn

Read It Together   Find the hat and the hand.

Phonics

Letter and Sound Tt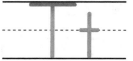

Write the missing letter. Color each item named in the sentence.

1. ___ten	**2.** ___itt	**3.** ___ape
4. ___ock	**5.** ___ub	**6.** ___ire
7. ___orse	**8.** ___op	**9.** ___able

Read It Together Find the ten and the tub.

Handwriting

High Frequency Words

Trace each word two times and then write it.

find find find

has has has

have have have

his his his

mother mother mother

too too too

Name _____ Date _____

Cut out the pictures and the book. Fold the book on the solid lines. Paste an *m* picture on each page and write its name. Read the sentence and color what it names.

Read It Together

My M m Book

Find the man.

● **Cut out the pictures and the book. Fold the book on the solid lines. Paste an _s_ picture on each page and write its name. Read the sentence and color what it names.**

Read It Together

Find the Sun.

My S s Book

Cut out the pictures and the book. Fold the book on the solid lines. Paste an *h* picture on each page and write its name. Read the sentence and color what it names.

Read It Together

My H h Book

Find the hat.

Name _____ Date _____

● Cut out the pictures and the book. Fold the book on the solid lines. Paste a *t* picture on each page and write its name. Read the sentence and color what it names.

Read It Together

Find the tub.

My T t Book

✂

Name _____ Date _____

Organize Ideas

Write about what your family does together.

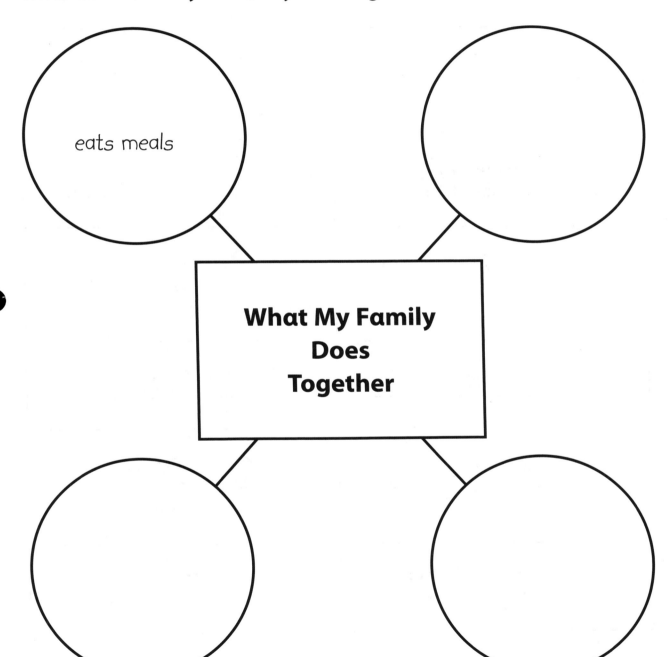

eats meals

What My Family Does Together

Name _____ Date _____

Phonics

Letter and Sound Aa

Write the missing letter. Color the item named in the sentence.

1.

apple

2.

op

3.

x

4.

ox

5.

lligator

6.

nt

Read It Together   Find the ax.

High Frequency Words

Find a Hat

Write a word from the box to complete each sentence.

High Frequency
Words
find
has
have
his
mother
too

_____
\- -

1. Sam _____ a hat.

_____
\- -

2. _____ hat is on the mat.

_____
\- -

3. His _____ sat on his hat!

_____
\- -

4. I have a hat, _____ .

_____
\- -

5. _____ my hat!

Name _____   Date _____

Grammar: Nouns

Use Nouns

1. Play Tic Tac Toe. Point to a square.

2. Say the word. Tell whether it names one or more than one person, place, or thing.

3. Use the word in a sentence.

4. If you choose the middle square, name your own noun. Complete steps 2 and 3.

5. Place your game marker in the square.

child	feet	woman
foot	Draw a noun. Name it.	men
man	women	children

Idea Web

Families in Many Cultures

Write about what families do together.

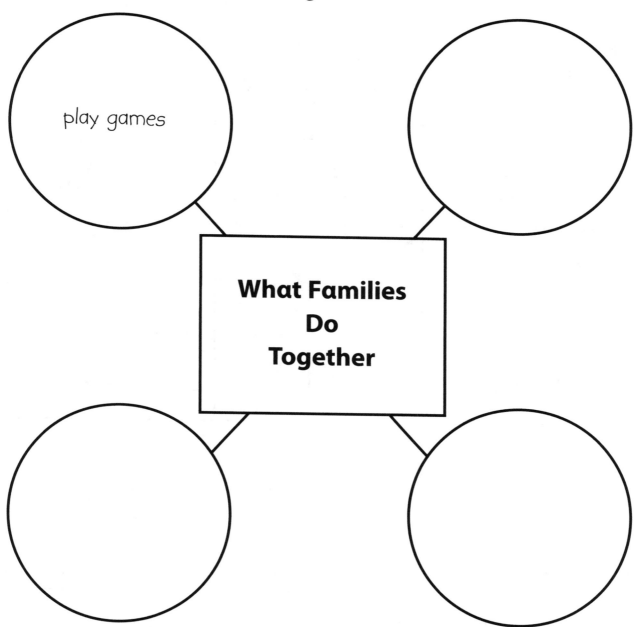

play games

What Families Do Together

Read It Together Take turns with a partner. Tell what you learned about families in "Families in Many Cultures."

Phonics

Letter and Sound Ff

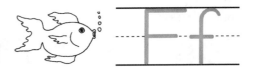

Write the missing letter. Color each item named in the sentence.

1. _f_ ox	2. _ ink	3. _ ork
4. _ ence	5. _ an	6. _ ive
7. _ oot	8. _ ish	9. _ ire

Read It Together   Find the fan and the fox.

Name _____ Date _____

Letter and Sound Nn

Write the missing letter. Color each item named in the sentence.

1. ___ut	**2.** ___en	**3.** ___ine
4. ___op	**5.** ___ail	**6.** ___est
7. ___et	**8.** ___ose	**9.** ___ox

Read It Together   Find a nut and a net.

Phonics

Letter and Sound Ll

 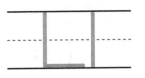

Write the missing letter. Color each item named in the sentence.

1.	2.	3.
__eg	__ub	__emon

4.	5.	6.
__eaf	__ape	__amb

7.	8.	9.
__orn	__og	__amp

Read It Together Find the leg and the log.

PM1.21

Phonics

Letter and Sound Pp

Write the missing letter. Color each item named in the sentence.

1. __ en	**2.** __ at	**3.** __ an
4. __ ear	**5.** __ eas	**6.** __ un
7. __ ire	**8.** __ illow	**9.** __ ot

Read It Together   Find the pan and the pot.

Name _____ Date _____

Letter and Sound Cc

Cc

Write the missing letter. Color each item named in the sentence.

1. cat	**2.** up	**3.** ix
4. an	**5.** ap	**6.** oot
7. ouse	**8.** orn	**9.** ow

Read It Together — Find the cat and the cap.

PM1.23 Unit 1 | My Family

 **Grammar**

Choose A or An

holiday	brother	egg
apple	friend	grandfather
sister	home	uncle
bed	orange	table
aunt	parent	meal
grandmother	banana	sister

Name _____ Date _____

High Frequency Words

Trace each word two times and then write it.

do do do

then then then

what what what

with with with

you you you

your your your

Cut out the pictures and the book. Fold the book on the solid lines. Paste an *f* picture on each page and write its name. Read the sentence and color what it names.

Cut out the pictures and the book. Fold the book on the solid lines. Paste an *n* picture on each page and write its name. Read the sentence and color what it names.

Read It Together

My N n Book

Find the nap.

Cut out the pictures and the book. Fold the book on the solid lines. Paste an *l* picture on each page and write its name. Read the sentence and color what it names.

Read It Together

Find the lamp.

My L l Book

Cut out the pictures and the book. Fold the book on the solid lines. Paste a *p* picture on each page and write its name. Read the sentence and color what it names.

Read It Together

My P p Book

Find the pan.

Cut out the pictures and the book. Fold the book on the solid lines. Paste a *c* picture on each page and write its name. Read the sentence and color what it names.

Read It Together

Find the can.

My C c Book

● High Frequency Word Cards

and	do
little	then
that	what
the	with
this	you
on	your

For use with TE p. T23g   **PM1.31**   Unit 1 | My Family

Grammar and Writing

Write Articles and Plural Nouns

1. **Read the story.**

2. **Circle the correct articles.**

3. **Fill in the blanks with plural nouns. Add -s or -es.**

It takes a lot of work to make (a/the) garden! First,

we cleaned up (a/the) yard. Then we moved two

_____

_____ (bench) near the garden. Next, we

_____

bought some seeds. I got _____ (bean) and

_____

_____ (sunflower). I also got (a/an)

apple seed. We planted (a/the) seeds. We watered them

with (a/an) hose. I can't wait to eat from (a/the) garden!

Vocabulary

Name It!

Grammar Rules Plural Nouns

- Add *s* to most nouns to show more than one.

  meal → meals

- Add *es* to nouns that end with *ss, x, ch,* and *sh* to show more than one.

  lunch → lunches

glass	sandwich	teacher	mother

meal		lunch

| **BEGIN** | | park |

| | | box |

| **END** | | |

brother	dish	class	bowl

1. Play with a partner.

2. Use a small object for a game piece.

3. Flip a coin.

   = Move 1 space.

   = Move 2 spaces.

4. Say the singular noun.

5. Write the plural form on another sheet of paper.

6. The first one to the END wins!

Name _____ Date _____

 Phonics

Letter and Sound Gg

_____
- - - - - - - - - - - - -
G g

Write the missing letter. Color each item named in the sentence.

1. girl	**2.** _up	**3.** _ift
4. _at	**5.** _ate	**6.** _uitar
7. _oat	**8.** _ion	**9.** _ink

Read It Together Find the gate and the goat.

Name _____   Date _____

Phonics

Letter and Sound Dd

Write the missing letter. Color each item named in the sentence.

1. dog	**2.** __oor	**3.** __esk
4. __ime	**5.** __ink	**6.** __uck
7. __irl	**8.** __oll	**9.** __eer

Read It Together   Find the duck and the door.

For use with TE p. T31o   **PM1.39**   Unit 1 | Family

● Cut out the pictures and the book. Fold the book on the solid lines. Paste an *r* picture on each page and write its name. Read the sentence and do what it says.

Read It Together

Put an X on the fan.

My R r Book

● High Frequency Word Cards

her	get
him	help
too	of
with	put
you	we
your	work

Setting Chart

Identify Setting

Write the setting of a family story you know at the top of the left column. Write about the setting below. Draw a picture of the setting in the right column.

Setting: _____	Picture of the Place

Phonics

Letter and Sound Oo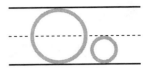

Write the missing letter. Put a dot by the item named.

1. ○strich	**2.** x
3. tter	**4.** nt
5. ish	**6.** live

Read It Together | Put a big dot by the ox.

A Big Help

Write a word from the box to complete each sentence.

High Frequency Words
get
help
of
put
we
work

1. I _____ with Mom.

2. We _____ a ham.

3. We _____ the ham in a pan.

4. My dog can _____ , too.

5. My dog can do a lot _____ work!

Name _____ Date _____

Use Proper Nouns

1. Point to a picture.

2. Use a common noun to name the place.

3. Then use a proper noun to name the place. Make up a name or use the name of a real place.

4. Say your sentences to your partner.

Cut out the pictures and the book. Fold the book on the solid lines. Paste an *o* picture on each page and write its name. Read the sentence and do what it says.

Read It Together

Put an X on the cap.

My O o Book

Name _____ Date _____

Final -s

Circle the word that completes each sentence and write it.

hat	hats

_____

1. Bob has lots of _____ .

has	his

_____

2. Bob _____ a dog, too.

has	is

_____

3. Rags _____ his dog.

get	gets

_____

4. Bob _____ Rags a hat.

his	is

_____

5. Rags likes _____ hat.

Grammar and Writing

Write Common and Proper Nouns

| state | dog | Shell Beach | brother | Miami | Ashley |

Look at each pair of sentences. Look at the <u>underlined word</u> in the first sentence. Draw a line to the common or proper noun that completes the second sentence.

1. This is my <u>sister</u>.

Her name is _____ .   brother

2. This is <u>James</u>.

He is my _____ .   Ashley

3. We live in a big <u>city</u>.

It is called _____ .   Miami

4. Miami is in <u>Florida</u>.

Our _____ is in the south.   state

5. We swim at the <u>beach</u>.

We often go to _____ .   dog

6. <u>Buddy</u> splashes in the waves

with us. Buddy is our _____ .   Shell Beach

Vocabulary

Family Trip Bingo

1. Write one Key Word in each suitcase.

2. Listen to the clues. Place a marker on the Key Word.

3. Say "Bingo" when you have four markers in a row.

Name _____ Date _____

Papá and Me

List the places that Papá and his son went. Then list words that tell what the places are like.

Places	What the Places are Like
• home	• fun
•	•
•	•
•	•

 Take turns with a partner. Use your setting chart to give information about the story.

Name _____ Date _____

Letter and Sound Bb

Write the missing letter. Color the item named in the sentence.

1. _ _ _ _ **b a t**	2. _ _ _ _ **u s**	3. _ _ _ _ **u n**
4. _ _ _ _ **a n**	5. _ _ _ _ **e d**	6. _ _ _ _ **a n**
7. _ _ _ _ **e e**	8. _ _ _ _ **i r d**	9. _ _ _ _ **o y**

Read It Together   Find the bed.

Name _____ Date _____

Letter and Sound Ww Ww

Write the missing letter. Color each item named in the sentence.

1.	**2.**	**3.**
w e b	ope	ave
4.	**5.**	**6.**
ell	ee	ing
7.	**8.**	**9.**
ig	ook	an

Read It Together   Find the wing and the well.

Phonics

Letter and Sound Jj

Write the missing letter. Put a dot on the item named.

1. jeans	**2.** __acket	**3.** __og
4. __eer	**5.** __et	**6.** __eal
7. __ion	**8.** __ar	**9.** __ips

Read It Together   Put a dot on the jet.

For use with TE p. T55m   **PM1.59**   **Unit 1** | My Family

Name _____ Date _____

Letter and Sound Zz Zz

Write the missing letter. Color each item named in the sentence.

1. tub	**2.** 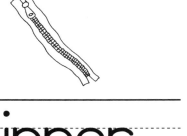 ipper
3.  ero	**4.** ase
5.  oo	**6.**  ock

Read It Together   Find the zoo and the zipper.

Grammar: Proper Nouns

Find Proper Nouns

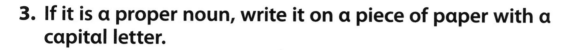

1. **Take turns with a partner.**

2. **Read the word in the box.**

3. **If it is a proper noun, write it on a piece of paper with a capital letter.**

4. **If it is a common noun, don't write anything.**

5. **Color all the boxes with a proper noun to get Fluffy to the vet.**

fluffy	nebraska	monday
home	trip	amy
idea	carlos	june
oak street	friday	share
october	group	visit
wisconsin	sunday	doctor dan

Name _____ Date _____

High Frequency Words

Trace each word two times and then write it.

day day day

from from from

good good good

she she she

us us us

very very very

Cut out the pictures and the book. Fold the book on the solid lines. Paste a *j* picture on each page and write its name. Read the sentence and do what it says.

Read It Together

Put an X on the hat.

My J j Book

Name _____ Date _____

Cut out the pictures and the book. Fold the book on the solid lines. Paste a *z* picture on each page and write its name. Read the sentence and do what it says.

Read It Together

Put an X on the wig.

My Z z Book

● High Frequency Word Cards

get	day
help	from
of	good
put	she
we	us
work	very

Phonics

Letter and Sound Ee Ee

Write the missing letter. Color each item named in the sentence.

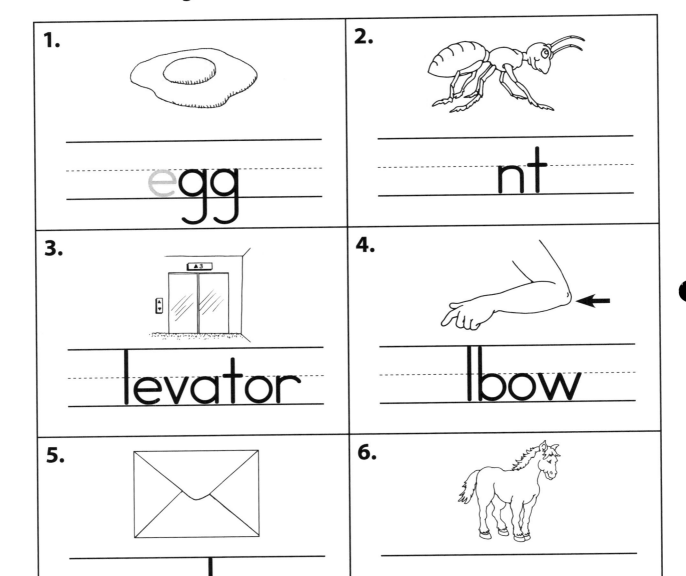

1. e_gg

2. _nt

3. _levator

4. _lbow

5. _nvelope

6. _orse

Read It Together   Find the egg and the elbow.

Name _____ Date _____

Zip Can Jog

Write a word from the box to complete each sentence.

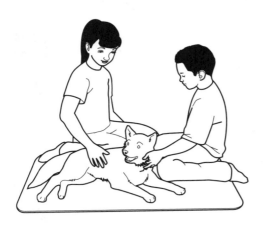

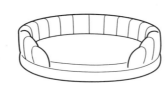

High Frequency Words
day
from
good
she
us
very

1. Zip is a _____ dog.

2. Zip can jog _____ the bed to the mat.

3. Zip can get a big pat from _____ .

4. _____ can jog from the mat to the bed.

5. Zip has a very good _____ !

Cut out the pictures and the book. Fold the book on the solid lines. Paste an *e* picture on each page and write its name. Read the sentence and do what it says.

Read It Together

Put an E on the leg.

My E e Book

Grammar and Writing

Proper Nouns and Dates

Look at each sentence. Circle the correct ending.

1. Jen lives in   seattle.

    Seattle.

2. She lives with her mom and her brother   Tim.

         tim.

3. Jen's family took a trip to   Texas.

         texas.

4. They left on   July 18 2013.

         July 18, 2013.

5. They came home the next   monday.

         Monday.

6. Jen learned that Texas can be very hot in   july!

         July!

Grammar: Proper Nouns

Name Game

Grammar Rules Proper Nouns

Start a proper noun
with a capital letter.   My dog <u>Mac</u> is the
best dog in the world.

1. **Play with a partner.**

2. **Spin the spinner.**

3. **Name a proper noun. Write the proper noun on a piece
   of paper.**

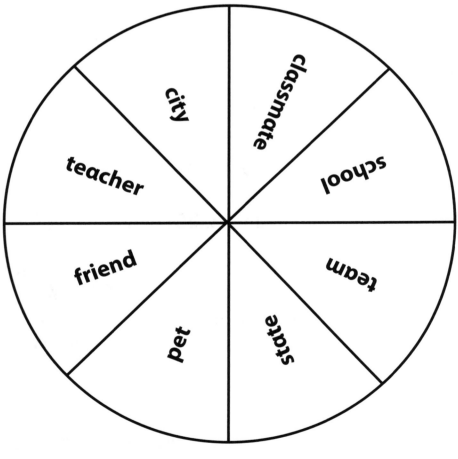

Make a Spinner

1. Put a paper clip
   ⬭ in the
   center of
   the circle.

2. Hold one end of
   the paper clip
   with a pencil.

3. Spin the paper
   clip around
   the pencil.

Prewrite Graphic Organizer: Idea Web

Idea Web

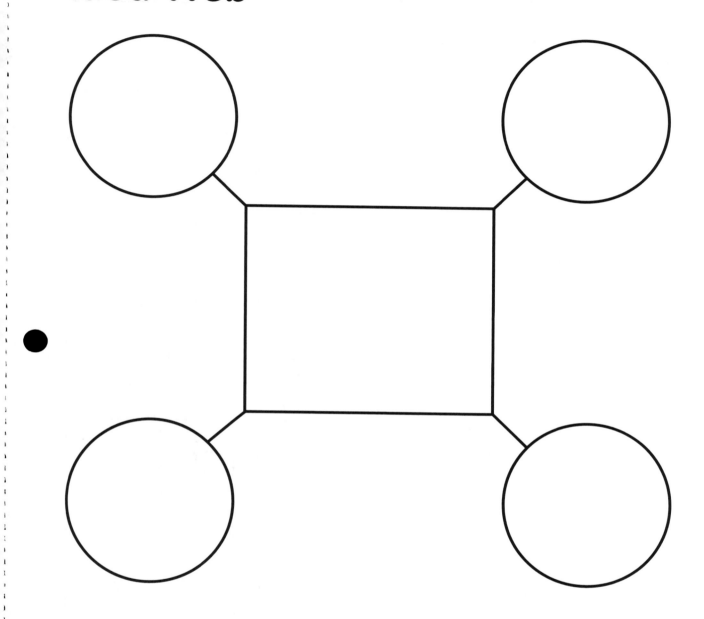

Word Choice Checklist

✓ Did you pick strong words?

✓ Do your words go with your pictures?

✓ Do your words grab your reader's attention?

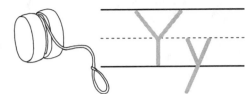

Phonics

Letter and Sound Yy

Name what is in each picture.
Write the missing letter.

1. _____ yarn	**2.** _____ olk
3. _____ amp	**4.** _____ acht
5. _____ ape	**6.** _____ ut

Read It Together   Can you find the nut? Yes, I can!

Name _____ Date _____

Letter and Sound Qq Qq

Name what is in each picture. Write the missing letter.

1. 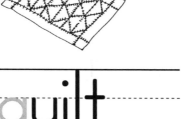 quilt	**2.**  ave
3.  ig	**4.**  uarter
5.  uart	**6.**  ing

Read It Together   Can I quit? Yes, you can.

Phonics

Letter and Sound Xx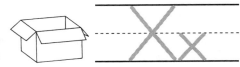

Cut out and name the picture cards. Trace the words. Put in the box the cards with names that end like *box*.

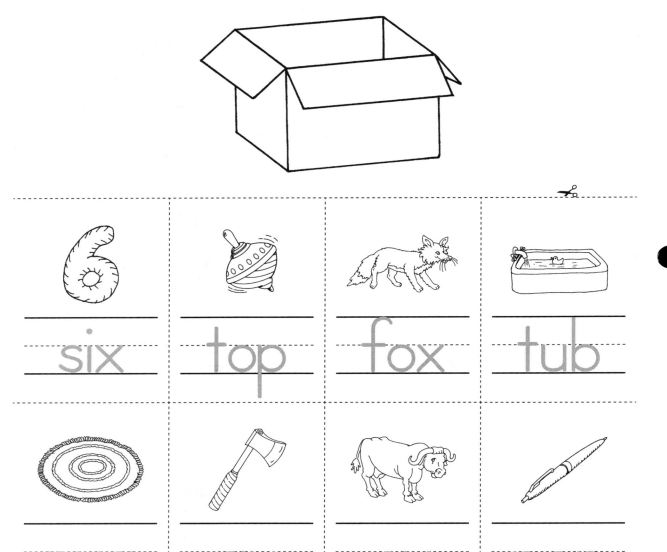

six   top   fox   tub

rug   ax   ox   pen

Read It Together   What is in your box?

Phonics

Letter and Sound Kk

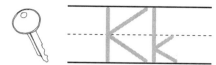

Name what is in each picture. Write the missing letter.

1. key	2. __obe	3. __it
4. __oll	5. __ing	6. __ox
7. __ite	8. __itten	9. r__ake

Read It Together Find the kit and the fox.

Name _____ Date _____

List Facts

Use the checklist. Decide if something is living or nonliving.

Living Things Checklist	
can eat	☐
can drink	☐
is healthy	☐
can think	☐

Words with 's

Circle the word that completes each sentence.
Write the word on the line. Read the sentences.

Sam	Sam's

----

1. What is in _____ box?

Jen	Jen's

----

2. Mom finds _____ cap in the box.

Dad	Dad's

----

3. _____ hat is in the box, too.

Quin	Quin's

----

4. _____ can not find his cat in the box.

Bev	Bev's

----

5. The cat naps on _____ mat.

Handwriting

High Frequency Words

Trace each word two times and then write it.

for for for

grow grow grow

keep keep keep

look look look

or or or

when when when

Cut out the pictures and the book. Fold the book on the solid lines. Paste a *y* picture on each page and write its name. Read the sentence and color what it names.

Read It Together

Find the yam.

My Y y Book

Name _____ Date _____

● **Cut out the pictures and the book. Fold the book on the solid lines. Paste a *q* picture on each page and write its name.**

Read It Together

Is this a Q?
Yes, it is a big Q!

Q

My Q q Book

Name _____ Date _____

Cut out the pictures and the book. Fold the book on the solid lines. Paste an *x* picture on each page and write its name. Draw a picture in the box that answers the question.

Read It Together

What do you have in a box?

My X x Book

Cut out the pictures and the book. Fold the book on the solid lines. Paste a *k* picture on each page and write its name. Read the sentence and color what it names.

Read It Together

Find the kid.

My K k Book

● High Frequency Word Cards

find	for
has	grow
have	keep
his	look
mother	or
too	when

Name _____ Date _____

Letter and Sound Uu

Uu

Name what is in each picture. Write the missing letter.

1. umpire	**2.** pple
3. ouse	**4.** nderwear
5. ncle	**6.** eal

Read It Together   Can a cub tug a tub in the mud?

Name _____ Date _____

It Can Grow!

Look at the pictures. Write a word from the box to complete each sentence.

High Frequency Words
for
grow
keep
look
or
when

_____

1. _____ can Jen get a pup?

2. This little pup is a good pup _____ Jen.

3. Jen can _____ this little pup!

4. Look at the little pup _____ !

5. Is it a little pup _____ a big dog?

Name _____   Date _____

● **Grammar: Adjectives**

Use Determiners

Cut out the words on the petals. Glue five petals around each center.
Then make sentences with the word in the center and each petal.

(that)   (those)

●   (these)   (this)

hat	gloves	garden	hose
plant	shoes	shirt	pants
socks	kittens	dog	rabbit
● glasses	pen	doors	window

● Cut out the pictures and the book. Fold the book on the solid lines. Paste a *u* picture on each page and write its name. Read the question and draw a picture.

Read It Together

Can a cub sit in the sun?

My U u Book

Grammar & Writing

Write Adjectives

Read the story. Then choose a word from the box that goes with the sentence. Write it on the line.

this	that	these	those	fat	green

Amy looked at the garden. "What is ___*that*___

thing over by the fence?" she asked her mom. On the

ground she saw a _____ green worm. Her

mom picked it up. She said, "_____ caterpillar

is fat. It likes to eat _____ plant stems. Her

mom pointed to the last row of tomatoes. "I found

many caterpillars on _____ plants!" Then she

looked down at the bean plants next to her feet. "I don't

think the caterpillars like to eat _____ beans,"

she said.

Vocabulary

Rivet

1. **Write the first letter of each word.**

2. **Have a partner try to guess the word.**

3. **Fill in letters one at a time until your partner guesses the word.**

1. __ __ __ __ __ __ __ __

2. __ __ __ __ __

3. __ __ __ __ __ __ __ __

4. __ __ __ __ __ __ __ __ __

5. __ __ __ __ __ __ __

6. __ __ __ __ __ __ __ __ __

7. __ __ __ __ __ __ __ __

8. __ __ __ __ __ __ __ __

9. __ __ __ __ __ __

10. __ __ __ __ __ __ __ __ __ __

11. __ __ __ __ __ __ __ __ __ __ __

 Take turns with a partner. Choose a word. Say it in a sentence.

Checklist

Are You Living?

Add facts you learned about living things to the checklist. Place checks in the boxes.

Living Things Checklist	
can eat	☐
can drink	☐
is healthy	☐
can think	☐
	☐
	☐
	☐
	☐

 Take turns with a partner. Tell a fact that you learned about living things in "Are You Living?"

Name _____   Date _____

Phonics

Double Consonants

we**ll**

Name what is in each picture. Draw a line from the first letter to the rest of the word. Write the word and read it.

1. og d ···· oll doll	**2.** uzz b oll	**3.** ill m itt
3. oss t iff	**5.** ell b ut	**6.** uff h ill

Read It Together What can you toss to a pal with a mitt?

Phonics

Double Consonants

Cut along the dotted lines. Write *t, b, l, m* in each box of one pull strip and *b, f, s, y* in each box of the other. Put the strips through the slits with the arrows pointing up. Read the words you make.

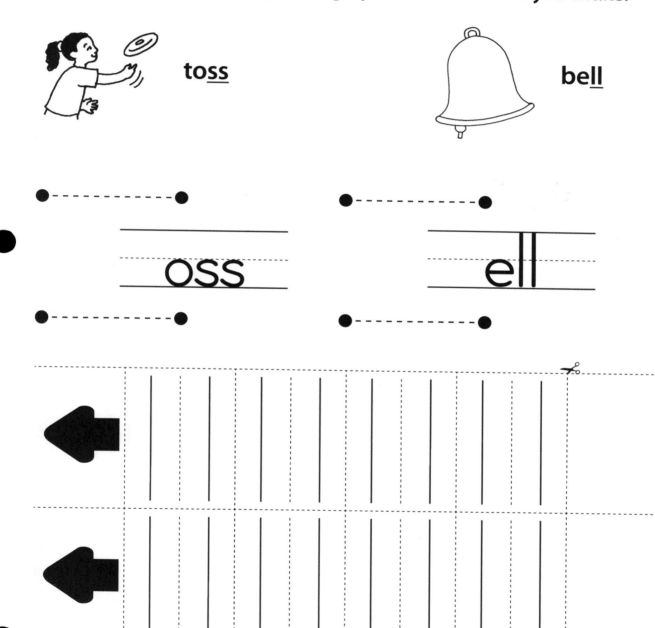

toss

bell

oss

ell

Phonics

Blend Words

Name what is in each picture. Circle the word that goes with the picture.

1.	**2.**	**3.**
bed (bell)	add egg	us up
4.	**5.**	**6.**
an man	wax well	box ox
7.	**8.**	**9.**
hill hat	is up	ill if

Read It Together Can you put a bell in a box?

PM2.22

Handwriting

High Frequency Words

Trace each word two times and then write it.

body body body

how how how

out out out

start start start

they they they

use use use

● Word Sort: Double Final Consonants

egg	bill	doll	cuff
pass	puff	buzz	hiss
tell	odd	fuzz	fill
off	lass	mess	dull
fell	muss	will	huff
well	add	mill	jazz
yell	kiss	fizz	pill

PM2.24

High Frequency Word Cards

do	body
then	how
what	out
with	start
you	they
your	use

For use with TE p. T87g   **PM2.25**   **Unit 2** | Shoot for the Sun

T-Chart

Compare Genres

Compare a song and a diagram.

Song	Diagram
	has numbered steps

 Work with a partner. Take turns asking about a song and a diagram.

Phonics

Words with <u>ck</u>, <u>ng</u>

duck

sing

Name what is in each picture. Circle the word that goes with each picture.

1.	2.
will (wing) wig	taps tan tack
3.	**4.**
sock sobs song	rip ring rock
5.	**6.**
kill kick king	loss lock long

Read It Together   A king has a ring. What has a wing?

High Frequency Words

Tug, Tug, Tug

Look at the picture.
Write a word from the box
to complete each sentence.

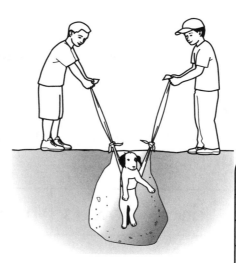

High Frequency Words

Words
body
how
out
start
they
use

1. The dog can not get _____ !

2. His _____ is too big.

3. _____ will the dog get out?

4. Tom and Tim _____ to help.

5. They _____ rags and tug, tug, tug!

Grammar: Adjectives

Use Shades of Meaning

Read the adjective below each box. Then draw a picture in the box to show something that the adjective may describe. Here are some ideas you can draw.

| apples | bugs | dogs | flowers | hats | shoes | trees | trucks |

small	**tiny**	**itsy-bitsy**
big	**huge**	**enormous**

Name _____ Date _____

Words with <u>ck</u>, <u>ng</u>

Cut along the dotted lines. Write *d, l, r, s* in each box of one pull strip and *k, r, s, w* in each box of the other. Put the strips through the slits with the arrows pointing up. Read the words you make.

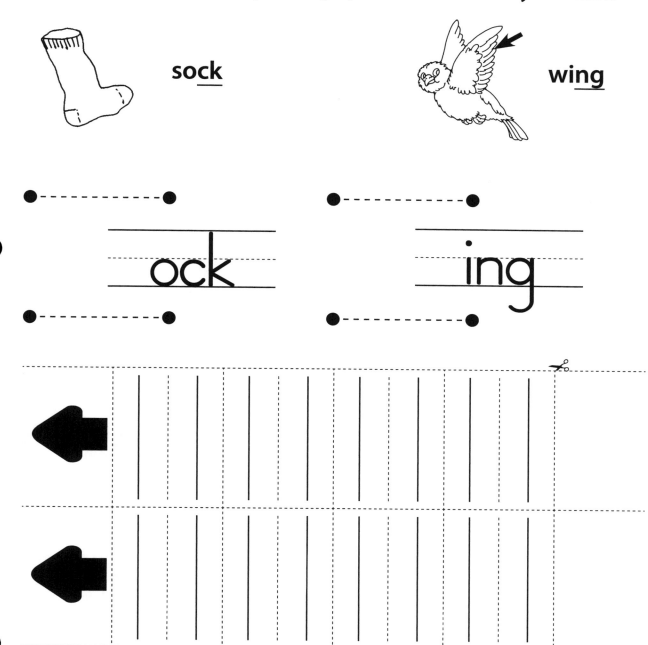

sock

wing

 <u>ock</u>

<u>ing</u>

Grammar & Writing

Write More Adjectives

Read the story. Then choose a word from the box that goes with the sentence. Write it on the line.

green	heavy	round	tiny

Jared and Paul planted a bag of seeds. "Wow,"

said Paul, "these seeds are so ___tiny___, I can

hardly see them." For a week, nothing happened. The

boys kept watering the seeds. The watering can was

_____

_____ and hard to lift. After a few weeks,

_____

they saw little _____ leaves coming out of the

soil. By the end of the month, they were eating delicious

_____

_____ radishes.

Grammar: Adjectives

Draw It!

Grammar Rules Adjectives

1. Adjectives describe how something looks.

2. Some adjectives tell about color, size, or shape.

    The green plant is tall.

Read each sentence. Draw a line under each adjective. Then use the sentences to draw a picture on a separate piece on paper.

1. The park has green grass and yellow flowers.

2. Children play with a big, red ball.

3. A small, brown bird flies above.

4. A boy sees a blue house with square windows.

5. A tall man sells round balloons in many colors and sizes.

Take turns with a partner. Show your picture and describe it.

Phonics

Blends f̲l̲, p̲l̲, s̲l̲

flag

plug

slot

Name what is in each picture. Circle the word that goes with each picture.

1.

flag

bag

wag

2.

us

fuss

plus

3.

led

sled

fled

4.

hum

slum

plum

5.

plug

lug

slug

6.

flock

lock

sock

Read It Together   Find a flag and a slug.

Name _____ Date _____

Identify Plot

Retell a story you know to a partner. Fill out the chart.

Title: _____

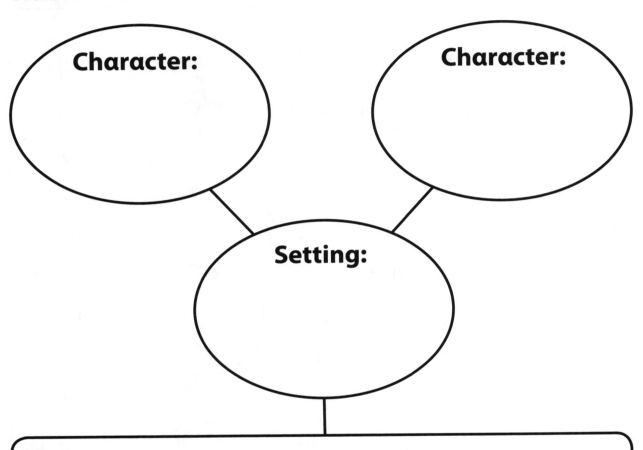

Character:

Character:

Setting:

Plot:

Phonics

Blends fl, pl, sl

Name what is in each picture. Draw a line from the blends on the left to the rest of the word. Write the word and read it.

1.	2.	3.
sl .... ed / ot	pl um / ug	fl at / ag
slot		

4.	5.	6.
pl us / uck	fl ock / ick	sl id / ug

Read It Together   Sid and Sam slid on the sled.

Name _____   Date _____

Blend words

Circle the word that names each picture. Read the word.

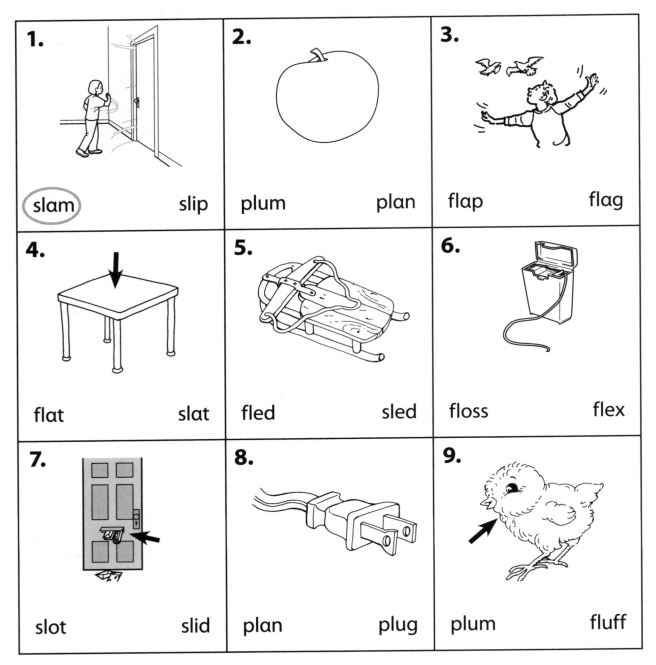

1. (slam) slip	**2.** plum plan	**3.** flap flag
4. flat slat	**5.** fled sled	**6.** floss flex
7. slot slid	**8.** plan plug	**9.** plum fluff

Read It Together   It is flat. Can it flap?

Handwriting

High Frequency Words

Trace each word two times and then write it.

does does does

eat eat eat

live live live

no no no

see see see

why why why

Word Cards: *fl, pl, sl*

flag	plug	sled	flock
fling	flip	flat	slit
flap	plan	plum	slip
plus	flick	slick	slam
slap	slop	flop	fled
pluck	slim	fluff	slung
sling	plop	slug	fleck

● High Frequency Word Cards

get	does
help	eat
of	live
put	no
we	see
work	why

For use with TE p. T93i   **PM2.39**   Unit 2 | Shoot for the Sun

Name _____ Date _____

Blends <u>cl</u>, <u>gl</u>, <u>bl</u>

 <u>cl</u>ass

 <u>gl</u>ob

 <u>bl</u>ock

Circle the word that names each picture. Read the word.

1.

cap

flap

(clap)

2.

black

flack

back

3.

glad

lad

clad

4.

lock

clock

flock

5.

gas

class

glass

6.

click

block

flick

Read It Together Do you clap when you are glad?

PM2.40

Unit 2 | Shoot for the Sun

High Frequency Words

What Is It?

Look at the picture. Write a word from the box to complete each sentence.

High Frequency **Words**
does
eat
live
no
see
why

1. _____ it start in an egg? Yes!

2. Do you _____ it peck? Yes!

3. Yum! Will it _____ a bug? Yes!

4. Can it live in your bed? _____ , it can not!

5. _____ not? It is a hen!

● Word Cards: Adjectives

some	a lot	much	a little
many	a few	three	six
hat	glove	garden	water
● shovel	bread	dirt	air
plant	shoe	shirt	seed
wind	kitten	dog	rain
glasses	pen	food	furniture
● snow	plate	apple	banana

For use with TE p. T93l
Unit 2 | Shoot for the Sun

Phonics

Blends <u>cl</u>, <u>gl</u>, <u>bl</u>

Draw a line from the blend on the left to the rest of the word. Write the word and read it.

1.	**2.**	**3.**
cl ·········· ip iff	gl ad um	gl ob ad
clip		
4.	**5.**	**6.**
bl ot ess	cl am ub	bl ab uff

Read It Together   Do you use black blocks and clips in class?

Vocabulary

Around the World

1. **The traveler stands behind a challenger.**

2. **Listen to the clue. Find the Key Word and say it.**

3. **The first to answer correctly travels to the next student on the right. The first traveler to go all around the circle wins.**

KEY WORDS

seed	bud	petal	flower	leaf

CLUES

• a part of a plant that is the start of a flower

• the flat, green part of a plant

• the flat part of a flower

• a part of a plant that is small and grows into a new plant

• a part of a plant that has many petals

Name _____ Date _____

The Daisy

Complete the chart. Describe what happens to the little seed in "The Daisy."

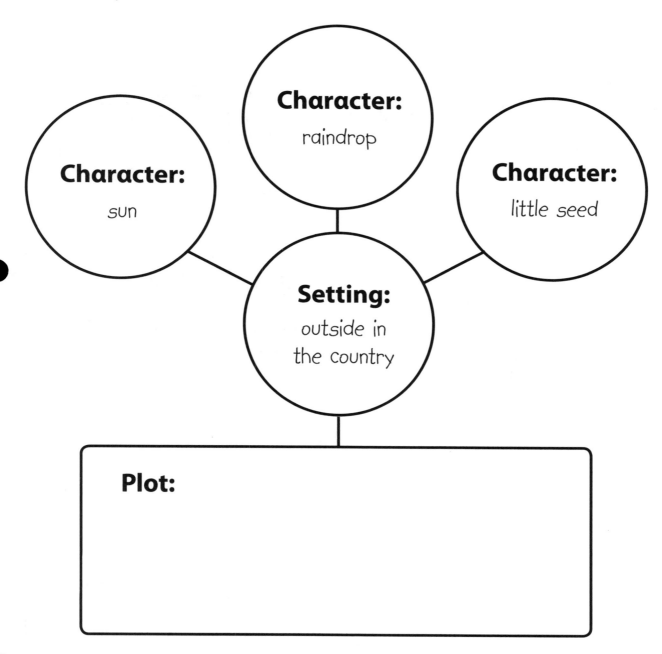

Character:
raindrop

Character:
sun

Character:
little seed

Setting:
outside in
the country

Plot:

 Take turns with a partner. Use your chart to describe what happens to the little seed.

Phonics

Blends fr, gr, tr

frog

grass

truck

Circle the word that goes with each picture. Read the word.

1.		2.	
	fog frog flag		track tuck pluck

3.		4.	
	trot frizz class		tap trap flap

5.		6.	
	gas glass grass		grub rub club

 **Read It Together**   We can see a grub in the grass.

Phonics

Blends fr, gr, tr

Draw a line from the blend on the left to the rest of the word.
Write the word and read it.

1.

ip
gr · · · · · · · · · · · · · · · · · · ·
in
_____
grin
_____

2.

ick
tr
uck
_____
_____

3.

ill
gr
id
_____
_____

4.

og
fr
izz
_____
_____

5.

ap
tr
ip
_____
_____

6.

ip
Gr
an
_____
_____

Read It Together   Tran trots to the truck.

Phonics

Blend words

Circle the word that goes with each picture. Read the word.

1. club (clam)	**2.** slug plug	**3.** clock click
4. plus plan	**5.** clog frog	**6.** plot glob
7. block black	**8.** grin grip	**9.** flag flat

Read It Together The black clock ticks and tocks.

PM2.50

Handwriting

High Frequency Words

Trace each word two times and then write it.

all all all

are are are

by by by

first first first

more more more

there there there

Word Cards: *fr, gr, tr, br, cr, dr* ●

frog	grass	truck	drop
frill	dress	drank	crop
grab	grow	grin	grunt
drill	crab	trim	trap
frizz	grub	gruff	drip
trip	grid	brim	brink
grip	crib	cram	Fred

For use with TE pp. T119g–T119h

● High Frequency Word Cards

day	all
from	are
good	by
she	first
us	more
very	there

For use with TE p. T119g

Unit 2 | Shoot for the Sun

T-Chart

Compare Genres

Compare a fairy tale and a project notebook.

Fairy Tale	Project Notebook
is a fantasy	is nonfiction

 Take turns with a partner. Tell how a fairy tale is different than a project notebook.

Name _____   Date _____

Blends <u>br</u>, <u>cr</u>, <u>dr</u>

brick

crab

drum

Circle the word that goes with each picture. Read the word.

1.

slim

grim

(brim)

2.

rib

crib

drill

3.

dress

press

brass

4.

grip

drop

crop

5.

tricks

bricks

clicks

6.

drip

grip

trip

Read It Together   Grab that brick, and do not drop it.

High Frequency Words

Yum!

Look at the pictures. Write a word from the box to complete each sentence.

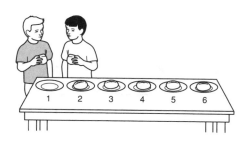
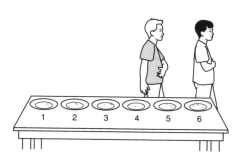

High Frequency **Words**
all
are
by
first
more
there

1. There _____ six buns.

2. Matt and Bill pass _____ the buns.

3. They eat the _____ bun.

4. Then they eat _____ the buns!

5. There are no _____ buns.

Grammar: Adjectives

Use Indefinite Adjectives

Use a number cube with six numbers to play the game. Roll the cube and find your number on the chart.

Chart

1	2	3	4	5	6
some	a few	a little	many	much	a lot

Say a sentence using the word that matches your number. If all of the players agree that your sentence is correct, mark it off on the score sheet.

Score Sheet

Player 1 _____ Player 2 _____ Player 3 _____

1		1		1	
2		2		2	
3		3		3	
4		4		4	
5		5		5	
6		6		6	

Phonics

Blends br, cr, dr

Draw a line from the blend on the left to the rest of the word.
Write the word and read it.

1.
 	
 X
 	
 cr ·········· ops
 ·········· oss
 _____
 cross
 _____
	2.
	
	 dr ag
	     ill
	 _____
	 _____
		3.
		
		 cr ib
		     ack
		 _____
		 _____

4.
 	
 dr   op
     ess
 _____
 _____
	5.
	
	 br icks
	     ag
	 _____
	 _____
		6.
		
		 br ing
		     im
		 _____
		 _____

Read It Together   Fred brings a brass drum.

Phonics

Short <u>o</u>, <u>e</u>, <u>u</u>

Circle the word that completes each sentence.
Write the word on the line. Read the sentences.

red   rod
_____

1. Fred has a little _____ hen.

clocks   clucks
_____

2. Fred's hen _____ a lot.

pecks   pucks
_____

3. It _____ in the mud, too.

begs   bugs
_____

4. The hen finds _____ to eat. Yum!

5. The hen does not like to eat

crops   cribs
_____

Fred's _____ !

Grammar & Writing

Write Indefinite Adjectives

Read the play. Then choose a word from the box that goes with each sentence.

some	a little	many	how many	how much

Kala is helping her father work in the family garden.

Father: Kala, please pour ___*a little*___ water on that row of beans. Not too much.

Kala: _____ plants look yellow and dry.

_____ rain do we need?

Father: I think three or four days of rain will really help our plants.

Kala: _____ hours have we been working in the sun?

Father: Maybe it's time to stop. Let's go get

_____ ice cream.

Grammar: Adjectives

At School

Grammar Rules Adjectives

1. Some adjectives tell how many there are of something.

   I ate <u>three</u> pears.

2. Some adjectives tell how much there is of something.

   I need <u>some</u> water.

Complete the sentences below. Use words from the box.

much	some	five	many	ten

1. There are __many__ books in the library.

2. There are _____ soccer balls in the gym.

3. There is _____ food in the cafeteria.

4. There is not _____ milk in the cafeteria.

5. There are _____ pencils on the desk.

💬 **Write two sentences about your school. Use adjectives. Read them to a partner.**

Name _____ Date _____

Steps in a Process Diagram

Materials: _____

_____

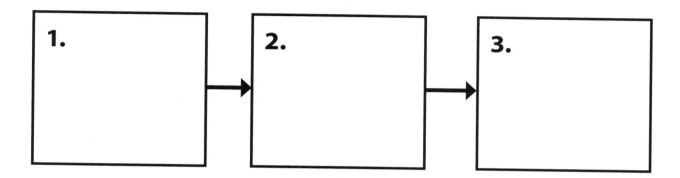

Organization Checklist

✓ Did you list what you need?
✓ Did you write what to do?
✓ Did you list the steps in order?
✓ Did you number the steps?

Phonics

Blends with s

spot

swing

sling

Circle the word that names each picture. Read and answer the question. Act out each action.

1.		2.	
	slim skim (swim)		spin grin skin

3.

sped
sled
slug

4.

steps
snaps
scabs

5.

snip
slip
skip

6.

spell
smell
swell

Read It Together   Can you skip, swim, spin, and sled?

Name _____ Date _____

Categorize Needs and Wants

List what you need and what you want in the T-chart below.

Need	Want
• peas	• toy car
• fish	• ball
•	•
•	•
•	•

Name _____ Date _____

Phonics

Blends with s

Draw a line from the first two letters to the rest of the word. Write the word and read it. Read the sentence.

1. ell / ot — sp → _spot_	**2.** im / ing — sw	**3.** em / op — st
4. ull / ip — sk	**5.** in / ill — sp	**6.** ing / ug — sl

Read It Together Stan sees a slug on the swing.

© National Geographic Learning, a part of Cengage Learning, Inc.
For use with TE p. T136f   **PM3.3**   Unit 3 | To Your Front Door

Handwriting

High Frequency Words

Trace each word two times and then write it.

go go go

great great great

one one one

saw saw saw

want want want

would would would

Word Cards: Words with *s* Blends ●

stack	snack	swim	sled
smack	spot	skill	swamp
step	smell	sling	skip
spill	swell	skid	stem ●
spend	skin	slam	smart
swing	slid	spin	sniff
snap	snug	stuck	small ●

● High Frequency Word Cards

for	go
grow	great
keep	one
look	saw
or	want
when	would

For use with TE p. T131k

PM3.6

Name _____ Date _____

Triple Blends with <u>s</u>

string

Circle the word that names the picture. Read the sentence.

1. snub (scrub) sub	**2.** snip scram strum
3. spring sling string	**4.** strong scram swing
5. slug sprig sprung	**6.** scrap stuck struck

Read It Together   The strong cat springs to get the string.

For use with TE p. T137e   **PM3.7**   **Unit 3** | To Your Front Door

High Frequency Words

The Sled

Look at the picture. Write a word from the box to complete each sentence.

High Frequency **Words**
go
great
one
saw
want
would

_____

1. What did I see? I _____ sleds on a hill.

_____

2. My pal slid on _____ sled.

_____

3. I _____ to get a sled, too.

_____

4. I _____ get on it and go, go, go!

_____

5. I would have _____ fun on my sled!

Name _____ Date _____

Use Action Verbs

1. Toss two markers on the game board. Toss one marker on the left side and one marker on the right side.

2. Say the word or words on the left. Name the action in the picture on the right.

3. Use the words in a sentence.

4. Play until each player has said five sentences.

He	
She	
The boy	
The Girl	
The man	
The woman	
The apple	
It	

Phonics

Triple Blends with s̲

Name the picture. Draw a line from the first three letters to the rest of the word. Write the word and read it. Read and act out the sentences.

1. aps scr ········· ams _____ scraps _____	**2.** ess str ing _____ _____ _____	**3.** ing spr ig _____ _____ _____
4. ap str ut _____ _____ _____	**5.** uff scr ub _____ _____ _____	**6.** ung spr ig _____ _____ _____

Read It Together   Spring up. Scrub up. Strut off.

Phonics

Endings -s, -ing

Take one card. Find the person with a card that has the same word on it, even if that word has a different ending. Say the words and use them in a sentence.

kick	**kicks**
quack	**quacks**
smell	**smells**
swing	**swinging**
sniff	**sniffing**
duck	**ducking**

Grammar and Writing

Write Present Tense Verbs

Subject	Action Verb
I	eat
We	shop
You	buy
They	sell
The girls	walk
He	eats
She	sells
It	walks
The boy	buys
The tree	grows

Read each sentence. Circle the correct verb. Write the verb.

1. We _____ through the market.
   walk
   walks

2. The man _____ fruit.
   sell
   sells

3. Kate _____ an orange.
   buy
   buys

4. Tom and I _____ grapes.
   buy
   buys

5. Kate _____ her orange.
   eat
   eats

6. We _____ our grapes.
   eat
   eats

7. They _____ fast.
   disappear
   disappears

Name _____ Date _____

Rivet

1. **Write the first letter of each word.**

2. **Try to guess the word.**

3. **Fill in the other letters of the word.**

1. ____ ____ ____ ____ ____

2. ____ ____ ____ ____ ____

3. ____ ____ ____ ____ ____ ____

4. ____ ____ ____ ____ ____

5. ____ ____ ____

6. ____ ____ ____ ____ ____ ____ ____

7. ____ ____ ____ ____ ____

8. ____ ____ ____

9. ____ ____ ____ ____

10. ____ ____ ____ ____

 Take turns with a partner. Choose a word. Say it in a sentence.

T-chart

Markets

List types of markets that you read about. List what each market sells in the What It Sells column.

Type of Market	What It Sells
• fruit market	• bananas, pears, grapes
•	•
•	•
•	•

 Take turns with a partner. Tell what you learned about markets. Use your T-chart.

Final <u>nd</u>, <u>nk</u>, <u>nt</u>

ha<u>nd</u>   **si<u>nk</u>**   **te<u>nt</u>**

Circle the word that names the picture. Read and answer the question.

1. and / (ant) / ax	**2.** skunk / skin / skull
3. plant / plank / plan	**4.** pick / pink / pond
5. bend / bell / bed	**6.** back / bank / band

 **Read It Together**   Does Hank see a skunk or an ant by the pond?

Phonics

Final nd, nk, nt

Write the letters to complete the word. Read and answer the question.

1. si**nk**	**2.** te___
3. ha___	**4.** tru___
5. pla___	**6.** po___

Read It Together   Can you put a hand or a trunk in the sink?

Name _____ Date _____

High Frequency Words

Trace each word two times and then write it.

give give give

he he he

know know know

said said said

watch watch watch

who who who

Word Cards: Final Blends -nd, -nk, -nt, -st, -mp, -ft, -sk, -lt

hand	sink	tent	lamp
lift	honk	tank	best
mint	ask	cost	send
went	felt	gift	wilt
raft	pond	skunk	stamp
hint	melt	fast	stand
romp	whisk	mask	theft

● High Frequency Word Cards

body	give
how	he
out	know
start	said
they	watch
use	who

For use with TE p. T155g   **PM3.19**   **Unit 3** | To Your Front Door

More Final Blends

Write the letters to complete the words. Read and act out the sentences.

1.	2.
_____ me**l**t	_____ bu
3.	**4.**
_____ re	_____ ra
5.	**6.**
_____ ju	_____ fa

Read It Together   Jump and run fast. Then rest!

PM3.24

Name _____ Date _____

Ending -<u>ed</u>

Read the word. Add -*ed* and write the new word on the line. Read the sentence.

<u>**sprint**</u>

1. Pam _____ .

<u>**pass**</u>

2. She _____ it.

<u>**kick**</u>

3. Jess _____ .

<u>**jump**</u>

4. Hank _____ .

<u>**block**</u>

5. Hank _____ it.

Grammar & Writing

Write the Present Tense

1. Read each word in the word box.

2. Read each sentence. Write the correct word on the line in each sentence.

3. Use each word only once.

like	tell	read
washes	eats	mix

1. Sometimes, I _____ mix _____ pancakes for breakfast.

2. My sister _____ cereal every morning.

3. My dogs _____ a treat after their morning walk.

4. Mom and Dad sometimes _____ the newspaper.

5. You never _____ me what you want to eat.

6. My brother _____ everyone's cups after we eat breakfast.

Grammar: Present Tense Verbs

From Farm to Market

Grammar Rules Present Tense Verbs	
Tell what one person or thing does now.	Use *s* at the end of the verb.
Marta *sells* fruit.	

Read each sentence. Circle the correct word. Write the word.

1. The farm ___*grows*___ flowers.   grow
                                      grows

2. Leo and Rita _____ flowers.   grow
                                        grows

3. The woman _____ flowers.   sell
                                     sells

4. Kyle and Eva _____ flowers.   sell
                                        sells

5. Mom _____ flowers.   buy
                               buys

6. Andy and Jorge _____ flowers.   buy
                                          buys

Make a list of verbs with a partner. Write a sentence with one verb for your partner to read aloud.

Name _____   Date _____

Words with <u>ch</u>, <u>tch</u>

<u>ch</u>in

Circle the word that names the picture.
Read and answer the question.

1.		2.	
	mask		chap
	mast		chest
	(match)		catch

3.		4.	
	batch		past
	bash		pats
	bench		patch

5.		6.	
	drink		crutch
	chin		crust
	win		club

Read It Together   Do you put a patch on pants or a bench?

PM3.28

Name _____ Date _____

Identify Details

Complete the Idea Web. Place one answer to the question in each circle.

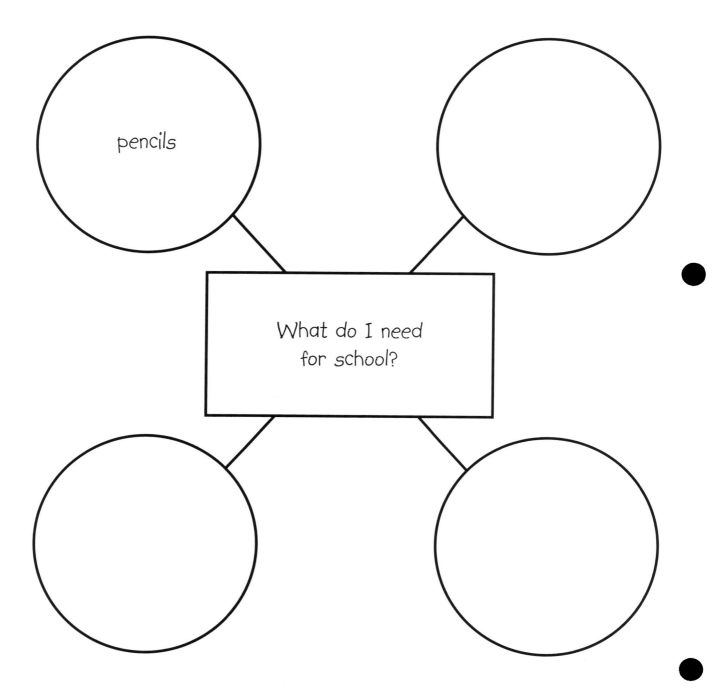

pencils

What do I need
for school?

Name _____ Date _____

Use *Am* and *Are*

1. Get a marker. Take turns with a partner.

2. Put your marker on a pronoun—**I**, **we**, or **you**.

3. Slide your marker to a verb—**am** or **are**.

4. Can you make a sentence? Get one point.
   (Hint: I am _____ . We are _____ . You are _____ .)

5. Now your partner gets a turn.

6. Play until both partners make five sentences.

are	am	are	am	are	am
I	We	You	We	I	You

Phonics

Words with <u>ch</u>, <u>tch</u>

Write the letters to complete the word. Read and answer the question.

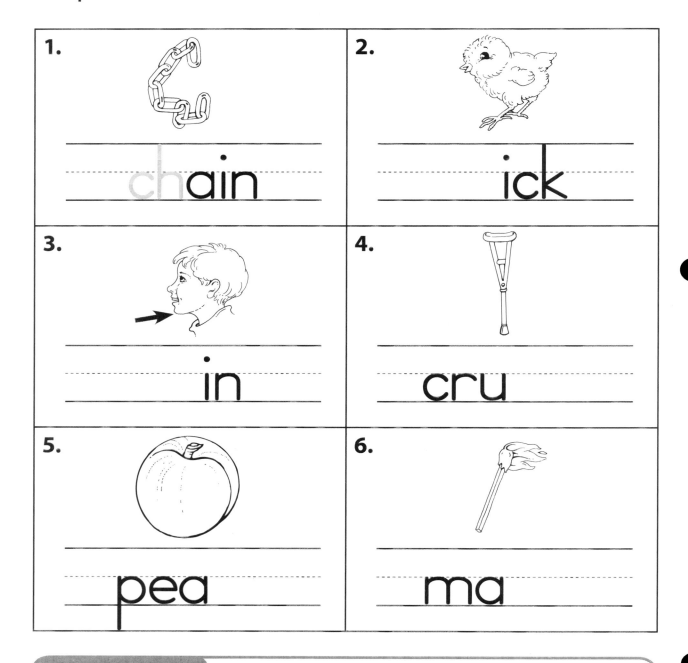

1. <u>ch</u>ain

2. ___ick

3. ___in

4. cru___

5. pea___

6. ma___

Read It Together Can a chick sit on a bench?

Phonics

Blend Words

Circle the word that names the picture. Read and answer the question.

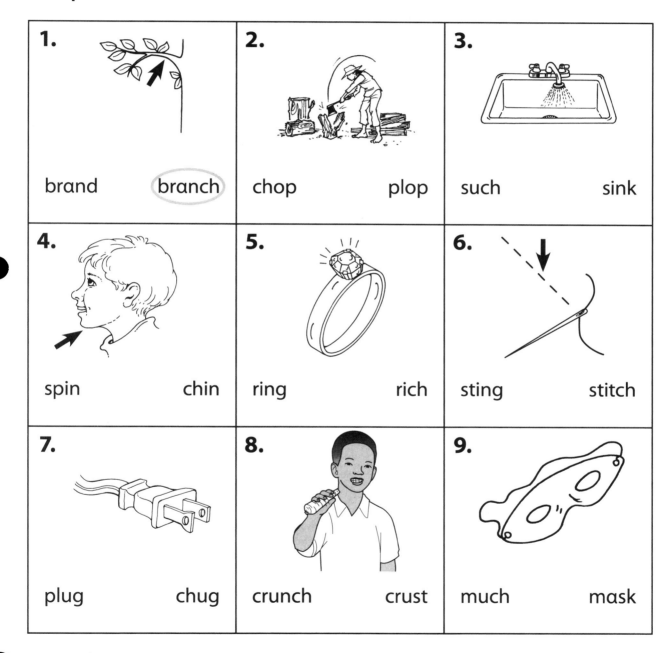

1.	brand (branch)
2.	chop plop
3.	such sink
4.	spin chin
5.	ring rich
6.	sting stitch
7.	plug chug
8.	crunch crust
9.	much mask

Read It Together   How much of the branch will he chop up?

Handwriting

High Frequency Words

Trace each word two times and then write it.

around around around

be be be

here here here

need need need

together together

together

where where where

● Word Cards: *ch, tch, th*

lunch	watch	cloth	chick
chop	thump	hatch	thick
thing	chill	ranch	that
pitch	check	catch	such
path	itch	patch	with
chest	rich	chat	witch
batch	chin	math	much

● High Frequency Word Cards

does	around
eat	be
live	here
no	need
see	together
why	where

Name _____ Date _____

Words with <u>th</u>

Circle the word that names the picture. Read the sentence.

1.

(think)

sink

drink

2.

chin

thin

tin

3.

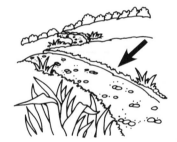

pan

that

path

4.

band

bath

bank

5.

then

test

tent

6.

tank

thank

than

Read It Together   Thad can thank Ruth for this.

Name _____   Date _____

Fetch It!

Look at the picture. Write a word from the box to complete each sentence. Read the sentence.

High Frequency **Words**
around
be
here
need
together
where

_____

- -

1. My dogs and I are at the pond _____ .

_____

- -

2. I toss a stick, and they _____ to find it.

_____

- -

3. My dogs sniff all _____ . They can not find the stick!

_____

- -

4. _____ can the stick be?

_____

- -

5. Look! It is _____ in the sand by the big rock!

Phonics

Words with th

Write the letters to complete each word. Read and answer the questions.

1. th**imble**	**2.** __ink
3. __tee	**4.** __in
5. ba__	**6.** umb__

Read It Together Does a dog want a bath? What do you think?

Name _____ Date _____

Phonics

Blend Words

Circle the word that names the picture. Read and answer
the question.

1.	2.	3.
(thick) chick	moth much	thin chin

4.	5.	6.
chomp them	math match	cloth clutch

7.	8.	9.
thump chump	think chimp	patch path

Read It Together Do you think that math is fun?

● **Grammar and Writing**

Be and the Present Progressive

1. **Read the words in the box.**

2. **Then read the letter.**

3. **Write the words that correctly complete the sentences in the letter.**

4. **Use each word only once.**

are sitting	is waving	are
is saying	am writing	is

Dear Uncle Nick,

I _am writing_ to you today from summer camp. Camp

_____ a lot of fun. We work in the garden and learn about

food every day. My best friends here _____ Ann and Tess.

Right now, we _____ under a big tree near our cabin.

Ann _____ to you and Tess _____

hello. See you soon.

Love,

Ella

Name _____ Date _____

Vocabulary Bingo

1. **Write Key Words on the lines.**

2. **Listen to the clues. Place a marker on the Key Word.**

3. **Say "Bingo" when you have four markers in a row.**

_____ _____ _____ _____

_____ _____ _____ _____

_____ _____ _____ _____

_____ _____ _____ _____

Name _____   Date _____

Idea Web

Delivery

Complete the Idea Web using details from "Delivery."

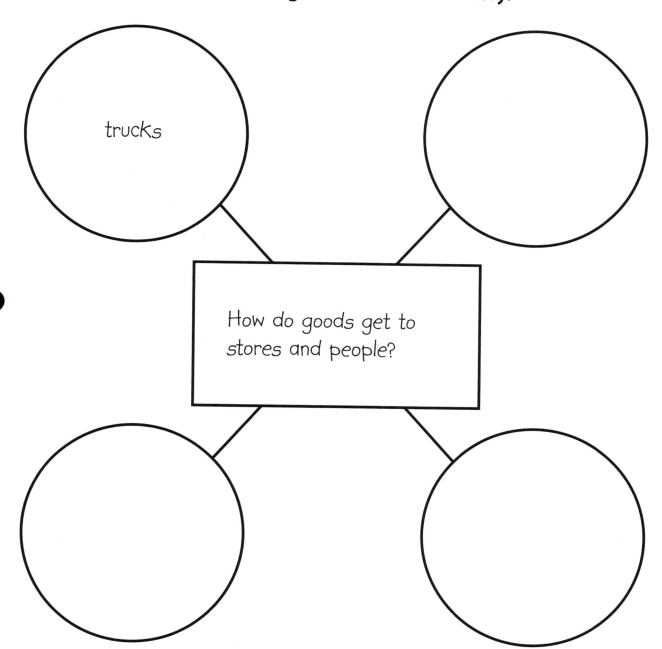

trucks

How do goods get to stores and people?

 Use your Idea Web to retell the poem to a partner.

Phonics

Words with <u>wh</u>

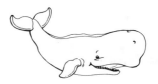

Circle the word that names the picture. Read and answer the question.

1. thank / check / (whack)	**2.** chin / when / thin
3. whisk / thick / chuck	**4.** chip / whip / with
5. which / chick / think	**6.** whiff / cliff / fifth

Read It Together   Do you use a whiff or a whisk when you mix?

Words with <u>wh</u>

Write the letters to complete the word. Read and answer the question.

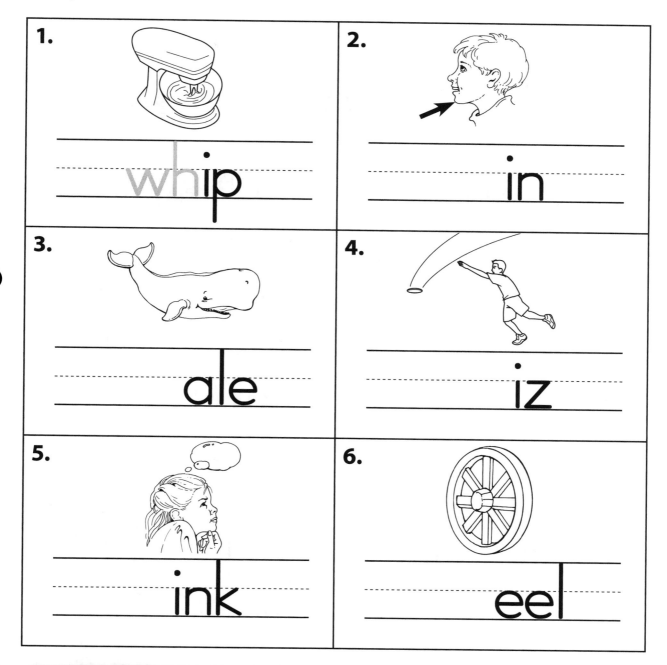

1. wh ip

2. in

3. ale

4. iz

5. ink

6. eel

Read It Together What can you see whiz by when you go out?

Name _____ Date _____

Phonics

Blend Words

Circle the word that names the picture. Read and answer the question.

1. think · whisk	**2.** which · chimp	**3.** check · what
4. with · whip	**5.** thank · when	**6.** whim · whiff
7. wham · chat	**8.** whack · wing	**9.** chop · whiz

Read It Together What can you whack with a bat?

© National Geographic Learning, a part of Cengage Learning, Inc.
For use with TE p. T193c   **PM3.45**   Unit 3 | To Your Front Door

Name _____ Date _____

High Frequency Words

Trace each word two times and then write it.

● come come come

found found found

● full full full

next next next

their their their

walk walk walk

●

Word Cards: *wh, sh*

whiff	ship	whale	shell
shy	whisk	why	shack
should	shin	which	where
mush	whim	she	whip
when	shall	wash	whomp
shed	what	wham	shop
wheel	shawl	whiz	dish

For use with TE p. T189g   **PM3.47**   Unit 3 | To Your Front Door

High Frequency Word Cards

all	come
are	found
by	full
first	next
more	their
there	walk

Name _____ Date _____

Idea Web

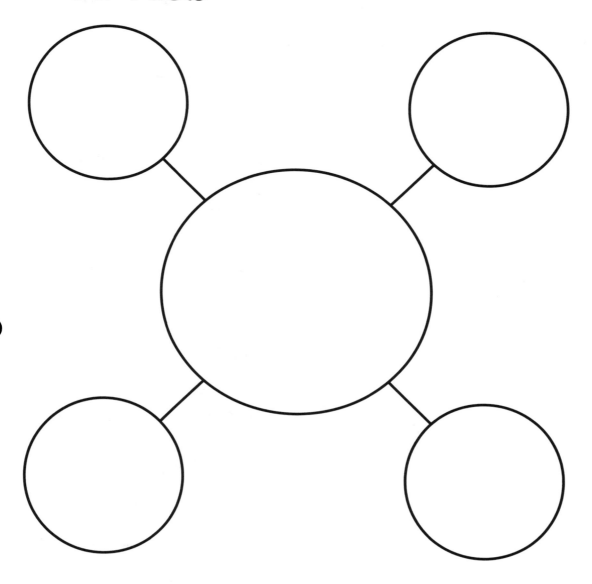

Voice Checklist

✓ Did you pick expressive words?
✓ Does your writing sound like you?
✓ Does your writing sound real?
✓ Do your words say what you want?

Phonics

Words with Long a

c<u>a</u>k<u>e</u>

Circle the word that names each picture.

1. rack / (rake) / rat	**2.** lane / lamp / long
3. game / gas / gum	**4.** bell / bake / bed
5. cape / cat / cut	**6.** got / get / gate
7. tap / tape / tack	**8.** wave / wax / well

Read It Together   Take the rake to the gate.

Beginning-Middle-End Chart

Identify Plot

Think of a story you know. Write or draw the plot in the chart.

Beginning:

Middle:

End:

Blend Words

Circle the word that names each picture.

1. cape   cake

2. brake   plate

3. grape   mane

4. cane   wave

5. scale   whale

6. skate   same

7. date   snake

8. save   flake

9. frame   plane

Read It Together   Would a whale or a snake be in a lake?

Phonics

Words with Long a

Complete each word so it names the picture.

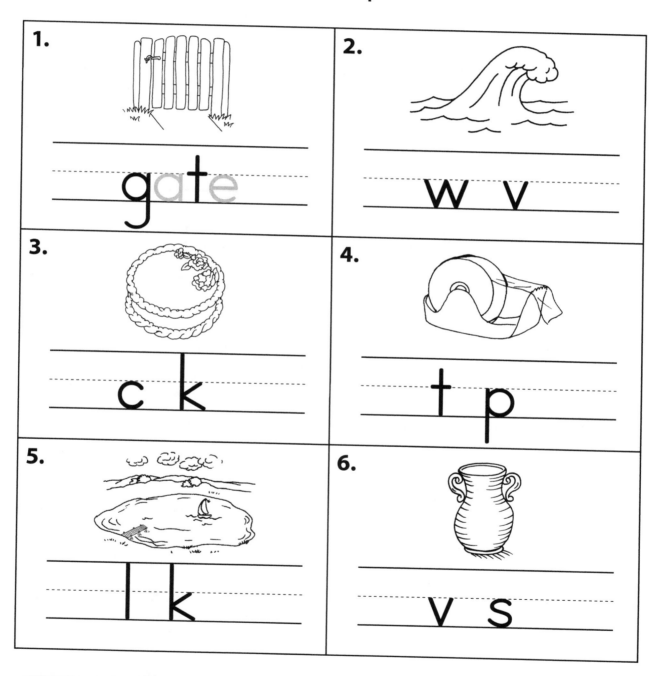

1. g a t e

2. w v

3. c k

4. t p

5. l k

6. v s

Read It Together Look at the waves in the lake.

Handwriting

High Frequency Words

Trace each word two times and then write it.

because because

because

carry carry carry

don't don't don't

new new new

play play play

sleep sleep sleep

• Long a Word Cards

snake	cane	game	gate
crate	bake	came	same
flame	cake	date	late
tame	wake	rake	mate
lane	lake	fame	rate
mane	flake	frame	plate
pane	take	plane	make

● High Frequency Word Cards

go	because
great	carry
one	don't
saw	new
want	play
would	sleep

For use with TE p. T199k **PM4.7** **Unit 4** | Growing and Changing

Name _____   Date _____

Phonics

Contractions

what + is	= what's
is + not	= isn't

Read the sentences. Write the contraction for the underlined words.

1. Can you see <u>what is</u> in the pond?

_____

Can you see _____ in the pond?

2. I <u>can not</u> see a cat in the pond.

_____

I _____ see a cat in the pond.

3. It <u>is not</u> a cat.

_____

It _____ a cat.

4. I think <u>it is</u> a fish!

_____

I think _____ a fish!

High Frequency Words

What's in the Box?

Write a word from the box to complete each sentence.

High Frequency **Words**
because
carry
don't
new
play
sleep

_____

1. Jack and Beth _____ have a dog.

_____

2. They _____ with Gramps's dog.

_____

3. They help Gramps _____ a box because it is big.

_____

4. What's in the box? A _____ pup is in it!

_____

5. They will play. Then the pup will _____ .

Word Cards: Subject Pronouns

I	you	he	she
it	we	you (more than one)	they
duck	Dad	you and your sister	Dave
eggs	Ali and I	Mom	pond
my cousins and I	duckling	desk	myself
pencils	you and your brothers	Ana	yourself

Phonics

Contractions

she	+ is	= she's
did	+ not	= didn't

Read the sentences. Write the contraction for the underlined words.

1. I <u>did not</u> see Jane. Did you?

_____

I _____ see Jane. Did you?

2. <u>She is</u> on the track.

_____

_____ on the track.

3. Jake <u>was not</u> on the track.

_____

Jake _____ on the track.

4. I think <u>he is</u> at bat.

_____

I think _____ at bat.

Grammar and Writing

Write Subject Pronouns

One	More Than One
I	**we**
you	**you**
he (for a male)	**they**
she (for a female)	**they**
it (for a thing or place)	**they**

Look at each pair of sentences. Look at the <u>underlined words</u> in the first sentence. Write the correct pronoun in the second sentence.

1. <u>Maya and Janet</u> look at the ducklings. _____ look at them every day.

2. <u>Maya</u> feeds the ducklings. _____ feeds them bread.

3. <u>Richard</u> walks around the pond. _____ walks quickly.

4. The <u>pond</u> is big. _____ is the ducks' home. [anno:] It

5. <u>My friend and I</u> watch the ducklings, too. _____ are happy to see them grow.

6. <u>You and your sister</u> must be quiet! _____ might scare the ducklings away.

Vocabulary Bingo

1. Write a Key Word in each egg.

2. Listen to the clues. Place a marker on the Key Word.

3. Say "Bingo" when you have four markers in a row.

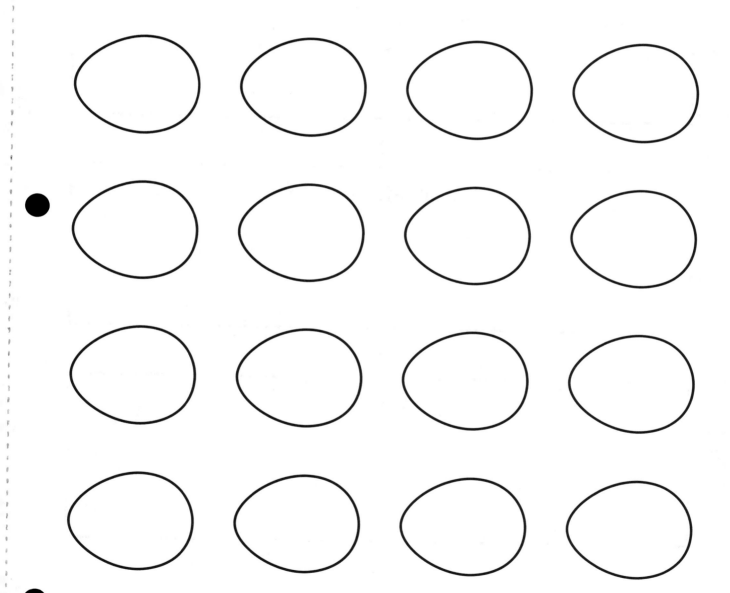

Beginning-Middle-End Chart

Ruby in Her Own Time

Complete the chart. Write the important parts of the plot from the story.

Beginning:

First, Ruby hatches from an egg.

Middle:

End:

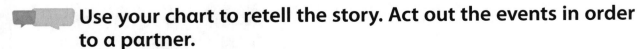 **Use your chart to retell the story. Act out the events in order to a partner.**

Phonics

Words with Long i

kite

Circle the word that names each picture.

1. fin / fan / (five)	**2.** back / bake / bike
3. lime / lip / lamp	**4.** dive / date / desk
5. date / dime / dim	**6.** name / nine / nest
7. him / hale / hive	**8.** bite / bib / brake

Read It Together Would you like five dimes or five limes?

Grammar

The Pronoun Game

1. Make a spinner.
2. Play with a partner.
3. Take turns spinning the spinner.
4. Say a sentence with the pronoun.

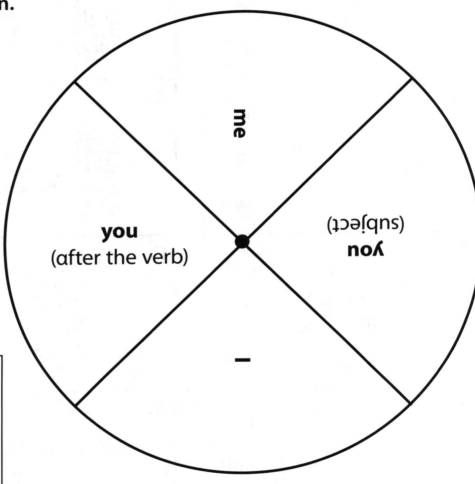

Make a Spinner

1. Put a paper clip 🖇 in the center of the circle.

2. Hold one end of the paper clip with a pencil.

3. Spin the paper clip around the pencil.

Name _____ Date _____

Blend Words

Circle the word that names the picture.

1.	**2.**	**3.**
tap (tape)	rid ride	can cane
4.	**5.**	**6.**
cap cape	dim dime	pin pine
7.	**8.**	**9.**
hat hate	kit kite	man mane

Read It Together Can a man ride a kite or a bike?

Phonics

Words with Long i

Complete each word so it names the picture.

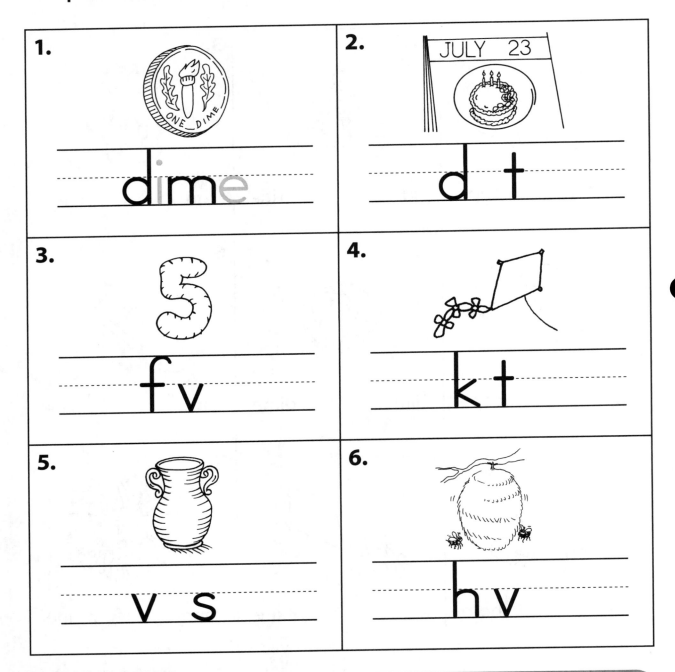

1. d**ime**	2. d t
3. f v	4. k t
5. v s	6. h v

Read It Together   Give me the kite and five dimes.

Handwriting

High Frequency Words

Trace each word two times and then write it.

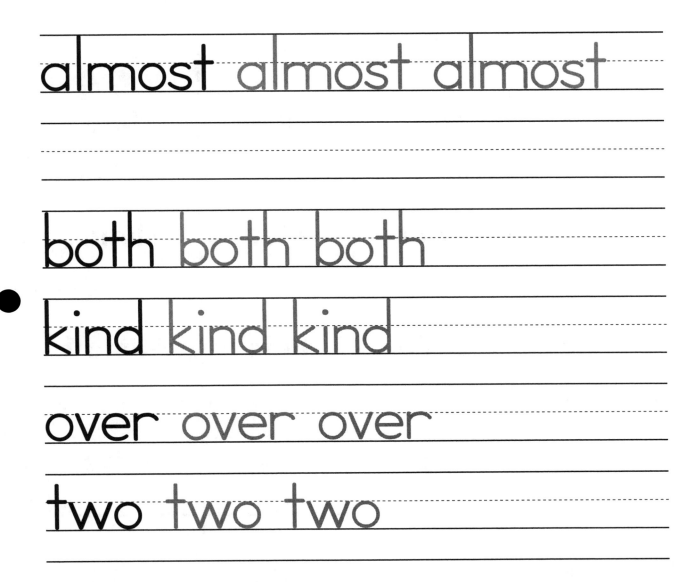

almost almost almost

both both both

kind kind kind

over over over

two two two

was was was

Long i Word Cards

bride	pile	time	five
smile	slide	dive	slide
mime	stride	hive	slime
hide	glide	hide	dime
file	tile	tide	thrive
wide	side	ride	strive
while	lime	drive	mile

PM4.20 **Unit 4** | Growing and Changing

Ending -<u>ed</u>

grin + n + ed = grinned
bake – e + ed = baked

Add the ending -*ed* to each word and write the new word.

grin
_____

1. He _____ .

bake
_____

2. He _____ .

clap
_____

3. She _____ .

smile
_____

4. He _____ .

Phonics

Ending -ing

| run + n + ing = running |
| bake − e + ing = baking |

Add the ending *-ing* to each word and write the new word.

jog
_____
- -

1. He is _____ .

dive
_____
- -

2. She is _____ .

swim
_____
- -

3. She is _____ .

wave
_____
- -

4. He is _____ .

High Frequency Words

At Bat

Write a word from the box to complete each sentence.

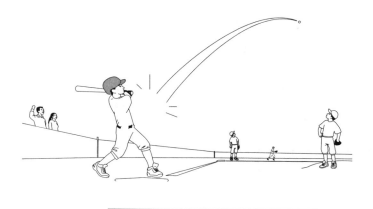

High Frequency Words
almost
both
kind
over
two
was

_____

1. Stan _____ at bat.

_____

2. He had _____ strikes.

_____

3. The pitch came. It was the _____ Stan liked.

_____

4. He hit it up _____ all the kids and almost out!

_____

5. _____ Mom and Dad clapped.

Grammar and Writing

Write Pronouns

Subject	After the Verb
I	me
you	you
he	him
she	her
it	it
they	them

Look at each pair of sentences. Look at the <u>underlined words</u> in the first sentence. Write the correct pronoun in the second sentence.

1. Dave, Joe, and Ana watch <u>the turtles</u>. They watch
   _____them_____ every day.

2. <u>Dave, Joe, and Ana</u> want to help them. _____ decide
   to feed them.

3. Dave feeds <u>one turtle</u>. He feeds _____ too much.

4. <u>Joe</u> meets <u>Dave</u> on the beach. _____ meets _____
   at 4 p.m.

5. Joe sees <u>Ana</u> on the beach. He sees _____ on the sand.

6. <u>I</u> can't use all the turtle food. Please don't give _____
   any more.

Ending -ed

Circle the word that
completes each sentence
and write it.

hugged   **hiked**
_____

----

1. Zane _____ up the path.

lugged   **liked**
_____

----

2. He _____ to sing.

hummed   **hated**
_____

----

3. He _____ a song as he walked.

jogged   **jabbed**
_____

----

4. Jen _____ by Zane.

chopped   **chimed**
_____

----

5. She _____ in and sang with him.

Name _____ Date _____

Phonics

Words with Long o

 r<u>o</u>p<u>e</u>

Circle the word that names each picture.

1. not (nose) name	**2.** hate hat hose
3. cone cane can	**4.** rake rack robe
5. name nap not	**6.** box bone band
7. run rock rose	**8.** hot home hand

Read It Together   The hose is by the roses at home.

● Long o Word Cards

cold	hole	bone	hose
nose	cone	gold	hold
close	pole	stone	phone
● sold	rose	mold	bold
stole	pose	zone	mole
fold	role	shone	those
● told	whole	lone	zone

High Frequency Word Cards

around	always
be	any
here	each
need	every
together	many
where	never

Phonics

More Words with Long o

Complete each word so it names the picture.

1. n o	**2.** ph__n
3. c__k	**4.** __g
5. pr__	**6.** __J

Read It Together   Jo wants to go see the pro play.

High Frequency Words
Do You Have a Pet?

Write a word from the box to complete each sentence.

High Frequency **Words**
always
any
each
every
many
never

1. How _____ kids in each class have pets?

2. We went to _____ class and asked.

3. We _____ asked kids with pets to stand.

4. Did _____ class not have pets?

5. No. We _____ found a class with no pets!

Word Sort: Possessive Nouns

1. Read each word in the top boxes.
2. Decide whether the word names one owner or more than one owner.
3. Write the word in the correct column of the chart.
4. Once all the words have been sorted, take turns using each one in a sentence.

girls'	spider's	butterfly's	chicks'
eggs'	Mario's	baby's	cocoons'

One Owner	More Than One Owner

Name _____   Date _____

More Words with Long o

Circle the word that completes each sentence and write it.

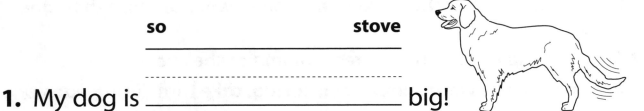

so   stove

_____

- -

1. My dog is _____ big!

Bo   nose

_____

- -

2. He's white with a black _____ .

go   got

_____

- -

3. He can _____ very fast.

No   Note

_____

- -

4. But he stops when I say, " _____ ."

pro   phone

_____

- -

5. I am a _____ with my big dog!

Name _____ Date _____

Write Possessive Nouns

One Owner	More Than One Owner
boy's	boys'
cat's	cats'
egg's	eggs'
caterpillar's	caterpillars'

Look at each pair of sentences. Look at the <u>underlined words</u> in the first sentence. Write the correct pronoun in the second sentence.

1. <u>The house of John</u> has a big backyard. _____ house has a big backyard.

2. We see <u>the nests of the birds</u> in the tree. We see _____ nests in the tree.

3. <u>The branches of the tree</u> protect the nests. The _____ branches protect the nests.

4. <u>The shells of the eggs</u> are thin but strong. The _____ shells are thin but strong.

5. Are <u>the eggs of the bird</u> ready to hatch? Are the _____ eggs ready to hatch?

6. <u>The beak of the baby</u> pokes through the egg. The _____ beak pokes through the egg.

Vocabulary

Yes or No?

1. Listen to the questions. Write the Key Word where it belongs in each sentence.

2. Listen to the questions again.

3. Check *yes* or *no* for each question.

	yes	no
	☐	☐

1. Can a _____ hang from a leaf?

2. Does a _____ stay the same as it grows? ☐ ☐

3. Can a _____ fly? ☐ ☐

4. Does a _____ lay eggs? ☐ ☐

5. Does every _____ have wings? ☐ ☐

6. Will you _____ as you grow? ☐ ☐

Name _____ Date _____

A Butterfly is Born

Write details in the chart that tell how a caterpillar changes into a butterfly.

Main Idea:
A caterpillar changes into a butterfly.

Detail:
hatches from an egg

Detail:

Detail:

Detail:

Detail:

Detail:

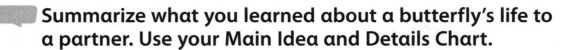 **Summarize what you learned about a butterfly's life to a partner. Use your Main Idea and Details Chart.**

Phonics

Words with u_e

Circle the word that
names each picture.

 c<u>u</u>b<u>e</u>

 t<u>u</u>b<u>e</u>

1.
mile

mole

(mule)

2.
June

just

jab

3.
rude

ride

rid

4.
fit

flat

flute

5.
cab

cube

cub

6.
prune

pane

pine

7.
dine

dune

den

8.
ten

tine

tune

Read It Together   Do you use a flute or a mule to play a tune?

Phonics

Words with u_e

Complete each word so it names the picture.

1. cube

2. f__s

3. m__t

4. t__p

5. m__l

6. p__l__m

Read It Together Does a block look like a fuse or a cube?

Handwriting

High Frequency Words

Trace each word two times and then write it.

four four four

may may may

only only only

other other other

show show show

some some some

Long u and Long e Word Cards

glue	meat	three	fruit
feel	suit	rescue	street
please	cute	these	tube
use	leaves	bean	huge
clue	peek	sneeze	teach
mule	due	flea	yeast
true	plume	beam	flute

● High Frequency Word Cards

come	four
found	may
full	only
next	other
their	show
walk	some

Name _____   Date _____

Compare Genres

Compare a science article and a poem.

Science Article	Poem
has real information	has information that is not real

 Tell a partner how a science article and a poem are different.

Phonics

Words with Long e

Complete each word so it names the picture.

1. __ h e

2. __ n

3. __ sh

4. __ w

5. St __ v

6. pr __

Read It Together   He is Steve, and she is Eve.

High Frequency Words

Math Time

Write a word from the box to complete each sentence.

High Frequency **Words**
four
may
only
other
show
some

1. I will _____ you some math.

2. Look! Two plus two is _____ .

3. Here is some _____ math.

4. You have two plums. _____ I have one?

5. Now you have _____ one plum, but I have one, too!

Grammar

Who Owns It?

1. **Toss a marker onto one of the sentence parts below.**

2. **Put it together with another sentence part. The noun or pronoun should match the possessive word.**

3. **Write the complete sentence on a separate piece of paper.**

4. **Say the sentence to your partner.**

We	spreads its wings.
watches her caterpillar.	I
Maria	crawl on our knees.
They	Juan and I
uses his hand lens.	take care of your chrysalis.
The butterfly	explore our backyard.
climbs the tree to find its food.	You
read my insect books.	lives in its habitat.
Maria and Juan	record their findings.
They	The caterpillar

Name _____   Date _____

Words with Long e

Circle the word that completes each
sentence and write it.

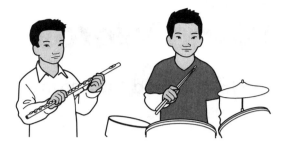

be   Pete
_____

- -

1. My best pal is _____ .

We   Theme
_____

- -

2. _____ play tunes together.

she   these
_____

- -

3. I play _____ drums.

He   Here
_____

- -

4. _____ plays that flute.

be   Steve
_____

- -

5. Will you _____ in a band with us?

Phonics

Blend Words

Circle the word that names each picture.

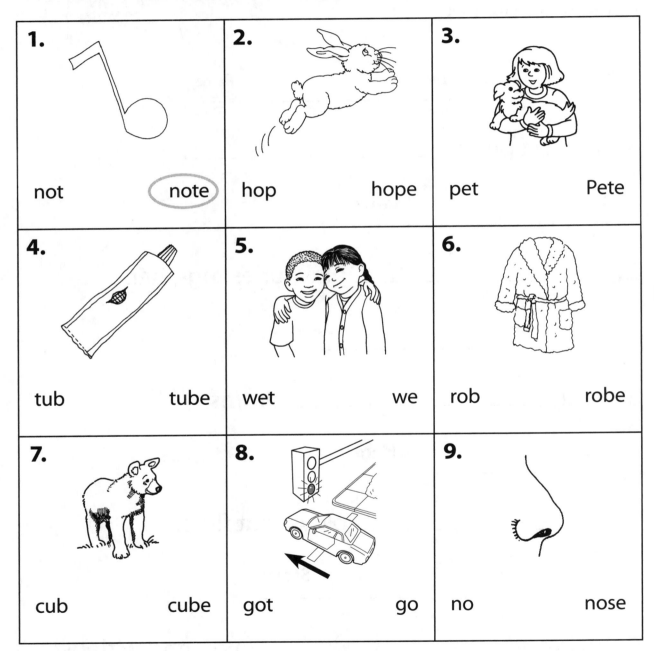

1. not ⟨note⟩	**2.** hop　　hope	**3.** pet　　Pete
4. tub　　tube	**5.** wet　　we	**6.** rob　　robe
7. cub　　cube	**8.** got　　go	**9.** no　　nose

Read It Together　A cute cub is not a good pet for Pete!

Grammar and Writing

Write Possessive Adjectives

Subject	Possessive Adjective
I	my
you	your
he	his
she	her
it	its
we	our
they	their

Look at each pair of sentences. Look at the <u>underlined words</u> in the first sentence. Write the correct pronoun in the second sentence.

1. <u>I</u> like to go exploring. I search in _____ backyard.

2. <u>Sara and Nate</u> came to visit. They wore _____ play clothes.

3. <u>We</u> crawled on the ground. It didn't matter if _____ clothes got dirty.

4. <u>Nate</u> wanted to see the insects. He brought _____ hand lens.

5. Sara found a <u>caterpillar</u>. We each looked at _____ striped back.

6. Do <u>you</u> like exploring, too? Next time bring _____ gear and come with us.